A Quiet Place

By Michele Spirn
Illustrated by Chi Chung

Scott Foresman
is an imprint of

Glenview, Illinois • Boston, Massachusetts • Chandler, Arizona •
Upper Saddle River, New Jersey

Illustrations

Chi Chung.

Photographs

Every effort has been made to secure permission and provide appropriate credit for photographic material. The publisher deeply regrets any omission and pledges to correct errors called to its attention in subsequent editions.

Unless otherwise acknowledged, all photographs are the property of Pearson Education, Inc.

19 Sophie James/Shutterstock.

ISBN 13: 978-0-328-50857-0
ISBN 10:   0-328-50857-8

14 16

"Look, Cindy," said Mom. "There's the Empire State Building."

Mom pointed at the tall landmark building up ahead. The skyscraper seemed to reach up to the sky. Suddenly, there was an unexpected blast of a car horn. It startled her. New York City was so noisy!

Mom smiled at Dad. "I can't believe we're here. Aren't we lucky that we moved to New York?"

She turned to Cindy. "You're going to have so much fun here."

Cindy sighed as she thought about their old home in Arizona. She remembered the quiet beauty of the West. She remembered the gentle whisper of the pine trees. She missed it all.

On every block, Cindy's mother found more buildings to admire. They all looked like tall slivers of metal and glass. It was hard to hear Mom, however. The street noise was so loud. Buses were roaring, and taxis and cars were honking. People were yelling. It was one big noisy package.

It was also hot, and Cindy's feet hurt from all the walking they had done. Cindy tried to imagine herself back home. She couldn't. Everything was making Cindy's head hurt.

"Can't we sit down somewhere?" she asked. "My feet hurt."

"Sure," Dad said. "My feet hurt, too, but this city is so exciting. I keep forgetting about my feet." He thought for a moment.

"I have an idea! Let's find a place to sit down and have a cold drink."

It took a while to find a place. If they had been back home, they would have gone to Lou's. Everyone knew them at Lou's. Lou would have mixed up one of his special drinks just for Cindy. She wouldn't even have had to ask.

Cindy hoped it would be quieter inside the restaurant, but it was just as noisy. People talked in loud voices. A radio played music so loud it seemed to crash into the room. Then, someone dropped a plate. Cindy jumped at the unexpected sound.

"What'll it be?" the waitress asked. She had to almost yell to be heard.

Cindy ordered one of the special fruit drinks listed on the menu. When it came, it was nothing like the ones Lou made. It wasn't special. Cindy pushed it away. Was there anything she would like in this strange, noisy city?

Dad guessed how Cindy felt.

"I am sure that all this feels strange to you," he said. "Don't worry. You just need to get your balance. This is a big city, and you're used to a small town."

"I don't like it here," Cindy said. "I wish we could go home."

"Try to adjust to life here, Cindy," Dad said. "You'll make new friends. Before you know it, you might even turn into a real New Yorker."

"Never," said Cindy. "This city is just too big and noisy."

The next day, Cindy and Mom went shopping.

"We have to get you some new clothes before school starts," Mom said.

In the store, Cindy looked at the racks of clothes. There was so much to choose from. It was all so fancy. At home, all she wore were jeans.

"What about jeans?" she asked.

"You can still wear those," Mom replied, "but you need some other clothes too."

That night Cindy put her new clothes away. It was nice to have new things, but Cindy wished she were wearing them back home. She looked out the window. Even seven floors up, she could still hear the honking horns and busy streets. New York City might be many things, but it would never be quiet and peaceful like back home.

Cindy got into bed and opened her favorite book, but she was too tired to read. Soon, she was asleep.

The next day, Mom said, "I have a surprise for you. I met our neighbors. They have a daughter your age. She'd like to meet you."

Cindy felt her heart beat faster. She was nervous. What if the girl didn't like her?

"What's her name?" Cindy asked.

"Lola," Mom answered.

The doorbell rang. Cindy gulped and went to open the door. Standing at the door was a girl with her mother. "You must be Cindy," the woman said. "This is my daughter, Lola."

Lola and her mother walked right in. The girl didn't wait for Cindy to speak. Instead, she started talking very fast.

"We thought we would show you around the neighborhood. Would you like that?" Lola asked.

"That would be great," Mom replied. "We would love that, wouldn't we, Cindy?"

Cindy tried to smile.

Lola started talking as soon as they got out of the apartment.

"Is it true you moved from out west? Did you have your own horse? Did you know any cowboys? Did you ever punch a cow? Can you rope a steer?"

Cindy laughed. Lola had strange ideas about the West. She told Lola about her old life and how she missed her friends and the quiet beauty.

"Have you always lived in New York City?" Cindy asked.

"Yup. I was born here," Lola said.

"How about some pizza?" Lola asked. "My mom said we'd treat."

They went into a pizza stand. They watched as a big man threw the dough into the air and twirled it around.

"Here comes trouble," he said as he smiled at Lola.

"Ray, this is my friend Cindy and her mother," Lola said. "They just moved here, and they need some real New York pizza."

"Four slices coming up."

The man took a wooden paddle and reached into the pizza oven. He pulled out a hot pie and began to cut it. Cindy was surprised to see that the pizza was served in separate slices, not as a whole big pie.

The pizza was good. Lola even showed Cindy how to fold it so that it didn't drip on her.

"Do you think you're going to like it here?" Lola asked. "It sure sounds different from where you came from."

"Maybe," Cindy said, "but I wish it weren't so noisy. Don't you ever want to go someplace quiet?"

"Not really," said Lola. "I'm used to it. I love the noise and the crowds."

"Dad says I just have to adjust," Cindy said. "Is it so bad to want a little peace and quiet now and then?"

Suddenly, Lola stopped eating. She quickly leaned over and whispered something in her mother's ear. Then her mother smiled.

"We know just the place to go. Finish eating your pizza, and we'll take you there."

They all finished quickly. Once outside, Cindy asked, "Where are we going?"

Lola smiled. "It's a surprise. You'll see. Hurry!"

She grabbed Cindy's hand and started running down the block. The mothers did their best to keep up.

They stopped in front of a handsome building. It looked different from the skyscrapers that Cindy had seen. It was old and made of stone. Instead of a glass door opening directly onto the sidewalk, the building had many steps leading up to the front. Cindy and Lola raced up the steps. Their mothers quickly joined them.

"What is this place?" Cindy asked.

"You'll see," said Lola. "It's just what you asked for."

She opened the door for everyone to enter. Cindy gasped. It was beautiful. Inside, there was a gold ceiling and beautiful brown wood all around. A woman was sitting at a front desk.

"Is this what you wanted?" Lola asked.

"Shush!" The woman at the desk raised her finger to tell them to be quiet.

"Oh, now I understand. It's a library!" said Cindy.

"You see," whispered Lola, "there are quiet places, even in New York City."

Cindy smiled. She knew she had found her quiet place. She also knew she had found a new friend.

Skyscrapers

The tall buildings we call skyscrapers got their name from ships. Tall masts on the ships were first called skyscrapers. When people began building tall buildings, they were called skyscrapers after the ships' masts.

New York City has the most skyscrapers of any city in the world.

The tallest building right now is located in Dubai. It is called the Burj Khalifa. It is 828 meters, or 2,716.5 feet high.

Many cities like to say they have the tallest skyscraper. Taller and taller buildings are being built all the time. Who knows how high the next skyscraper will be?

Burj Khalifa